LIBERATING YOURSELF FROM COMPULSIVE LYING BY UNMASKING THE TRUTH

100 QUESTIONS YOU MUST ASK YOURSELF TO AVOID LOSING EVERYTHING YOU'VE WORKED FOR BECAUSE OF YOUR PATHOLOGICAL LYING BEHAVIOR

DISCLAIMER

This book is designed to provide information only. This information is provided and sold with the knowledge that the publisher and author do not offer any legal or other professional advice. In the case of a need for any such expertise, consult with the appropriate professional.

This book does not contain all the information available on the subject. This book has not been created to be specific to any individual's or organization's situation or needs. Every effort has been made to make this book as accurate as possible. However, there may be typographical and or content errors. Therefore, this book should serve only as a general guide, not as the ultimate source of subject information.

This book contains information that might be dated and is intended only to educate and entertain. The author and publisher shall have no liability or responsibility to any person or entity regarding any loss or damage incurred or alleged to have incurred, directly or indirectly, by the information contained in this book.

Table of Contents

Introduction

In the heart of every truth is a journey. If you have found yourself on a path of deception, now is the time to bravely uncover the raw, sometimes unsettling reality of your compulsive lying.

In this groundbreaking book, "Unraveling Lies: Liberating Yourself From Compulsive Lying By Unmasking The Truth," you'll find a pathway back to your authentic self.

Herein lie a hundred questions, each one a stepping stone to self-reflection. These questions are more than mere words. They are invitations to delve deep, uncover your motives, fears, consequences, and the potential for change.

They challenge you to face the undercurrents of your behavior and push you to consider the impact of your actions on yourself and those around you.

With honesty as your guiding principle, embark on this introspective voyage to understand the whys, the whens, and the hows of your lying behavior. This book is not about blame; it's about acceptance, responsibility, and most importantly, transformation.

In every question lies an opportunity, a moment for introspection. Are you ready to embrace the uncomfortable? To break the cycle? To rebuild the bridges that may have been burnt by lies?

In this courageous exploration of self, you'll find the tools you need to step away from deception and move toward a more authentic life. So dive into this book and start your journey toward truth today.

The FAQ You Need To Understand What "Compulsive Lying Addiction" Is Really About

1. What is compulsive lying addiction?

Compulsive or pathological lying addiction is a behavior characterized by the persistent and habitual act of telling lies, even when there is no clear benefit or reason to do so. Unlike strategic lying or white lies, which most people occasionally tell, compulsive lying is uncontrollable and often unnecessary.

The individual may lie about both significant and insignificant matters, making it challenging to separate truths from fabrications.

2. What causes compulsive lying?

The causes of compulsive lying are complex and not completely understood. It's often a combination of factors, including genetic predisposition, childhood environment, and mental health conditions. Certain personality disorders, like antisocial personality disorder, borderline personality disorder, or narcissistic personality disorder, can be associated with compulsive lying.

Early childhood trauma or growing up in an environment where lying was normalized can also contribute to the development of this habit.

3. How does compulsive lying affect relationships?

Compulsive lying can profoundly impact relationships, leading to a breakdown of trust, which is a fundamental component of any healthy relationship. When a person consistently lies, it becomes difficult for others to believe them, even when they're telling the truth. This can lead to conflict, emotional distress, and betrayal. In extreme cases, relationships may end due to the erosion of trust and the emotional toll it takes on the other person.

4. Can compulsive lying be treated?

Yes, compulsive lying can be addressed through professional help, including psychotherapy, cognitive-behavioral therapy (CBT), or even medication in some cases. Psychotherapy can help an individual understand the root cause of their lying behavior. At the same time, CBT provides tools and techniques to change thought and behavior patterns.

However, it's important to note that the individual must be willing to recognize the issue and actively participate in the treatment process for it to be successful.

5. Is compulsive lying a symptom of another disorder?

Compulsive lying can be a symptom or characteristic of several mental health disorders. For example, it is often associated with personality disorders such as antisocial personality disorder, borderline personality disorder, and narcissistic personality disorder. It can also occur in conjunction with other disorders like bipolar disorder, ADHD, or addiction.

However, it's important to note that not everyone with these conditions will display compulsive lying behavior, and not every compulsive liar has an underlying mental health disorder.

6. What is the difference between compulsive lying and occasional lying?

Occasional lying is something that most people engage in from time to time. These lies often have a clear purpose, such as avoiding conflict or protecting someone's feelings. Compulsive lying, on the other hand, is a habitual behavior. Compulsive liars often lie without an apparent reason or benefit, and their lies can range from minor details to significant events or experiences. This chronic lying often leads to a web of deceit that can be challenging to maintain.

7. How can I tell if someone is a compulsive liar?

Identifying a compulsive liar can be difficult, as they often become adept at deceit. However, some signs may include frequent inconsistencies in their stories, lying about insignificant matters, or a pattern of deception that seems to serve no clear purpose. They may also show little remorse or discomfort when caught lying. Therefore, if you suspect someone is a compulsive liar, it's essential to approach the situation with empathy and encourage them to seek professional help.

8. How can I support someone struggling with compulsive lying?

Supporting someone with a compulsive lying issue can be challenging. Start by expressing your concerns in a non-judgmental and empathetic manner. Encourage them to seek professional help, such as a therapist or a counselor. Set clear boundaries regarding what you will tolerate in your relationship. Be patient, as change will not happen overnight. Remember, it's vital to protect your own emotional well-being too.

9. Can compulsive lying be a learned behavior?

While the exact cause of compulsive lying isn't known, it can be a learned behavior in some cases. For example, if a child grows up in an environment where lying is normalized or learns that it gets them attention, sympathy, or other forms of emotional reward, they might continue this behavior into adulthood. It can also serve as a coping mechanism to deal with stress, anxiety, or feelings of inadequacy.

10. Is there a relationship between compulsive lying and self-esteem?

Yes, there can be a relationship between compulsive lying and self-esteem. Some compulsive liars may lie to create a more favorable or impressive image of themselves, suggesting underlying issues with self-esteem. They may feel that the truth about their lives isn't good enough, and so they fabricate stories to feel better about themselves or to gain acceptance from others. However, this is not the case for all compulsive liars, and the relationship between compulsive lying and self-esteem can be complex.

11. Do compulsive liars feel guilt or remorse?

Feelings of guilt or remorse can vary widely among compulsive liars. Some may feel deep guilt or shame, especially if their lies hurt others or damaged relationships. However, others may not feel guilt or remorse, mainly if they've developed a habit of rationalizing their lies or if they have certain personality disorders associated with a lack of empathy.

12. Can compulsive lying affect a person's ability to trust others?

Yes, compulsive lying can affect a person's ability to trust others. If a person habitually lies, they may start to believe that others do the same, leading to skepticism and mistrust. Additionally, if a compulsive liar has experienced negative reactions or consequences when their lies have been uncovered, it could further erode their trust in others.

13. Can compulsive liars start to believe their own lies?

In some cases, compulsive liars can start to believe their own lies. This is known as confabulation. They may tell lies so frequently that they blur the line between reality and fabrication, making it difficult for them to distinguish between the two. This can create a complex web of deceit that even the liar begins to accept as truth.

14. What types of lies do compulsive liars tell?

Compulsive liars can tell a wide range of lies, from small embellishments to grandiose fabrications. These lies can be about anything - personal achievements, experiences, relationships, or even mundane everyday details. What differentiates compulsive liars is not so much the content of the lies, but the habitual and uncontrollable nature of the lying behavior.

15. Why do compulsive liars seek external validation?

Compulsive liars may seek external validation if they struggle with low self-esteem or a sense of inadequacy. By lying about their achievements, experiences, or abilities, they may hope to gain approval, admiration, or acceptance from others. However, this external validation is usually short-lived and can lead to a cycle of lying to maintain the false image they have created.

16. Can compulsive lying lead to legal consequences?

Yes, compulsive lying can lead to legal consequences if the lies fall within the purview of the law. For example, if a compulsive liar engages in fraudulent activities such as identity theft, falsifying documents, or perjury (lying under oath), they can face legal repercussions. In business and professional settings, lying about qualifications or financial data can also result in penalties. It's crucial to understand that while not all lies have legal consequences, they can undoubtedly damage personal and professional relationships and credibility.

17. Is compulsive lying considered a mental health disorder?

Compulsive lying itself is not officially recognized as a distinct mental health disorder in the Diagnostic and Statistical Manual of Mental Disorders (DSM-5). However, it's often associated with certain personality disorders such as antisocial or borderline personality disorder. It's also sometimes seen in conjunction with other mental health issues like anxiety and depression.

Therefore, compulsive lying is typically viewed more as a symptom or characteristic of other underlying disorders.

18. Does compulsive lying worsen over time?

If left unchecked, compulsive lying can indeed worsen over time. As the individual tells more lies, they may need to fabricate additional lies to maintain the deception. This can result in a complicated web of falsehoods that becomes increasingly difficult to manage.

Over time, this could lead to significant personal and professional consequences, including loss of trust, damaged relationships, and potentially legal trouble.

19. Can someone stop being a compulsive liar?

Absolutely. Overcoming compulsive lying is a process that involves self-awareness, understanding the root causes, and learning new coping mechanisms. Psychotherapy, particularly cognitive-behavioral therapy (CBT), can be particularly effective as it helps the individual understand the thoughts and feelings that lead to the lying behavior and develop healthier ways to respond to these triggers.

20. What is the first step to overcoming compulsive lying?

The first step to overcoming compulsive lying is often acknowledgment and acceptance of the problem. This involves recognizing the harmful effects of lying on oneself and others. Once this recognition occurs, the individual can seek professional help, such as a mental health counselor or therapist. Therapy can help the person understand the underlying reasons for their compulsive lying and equip them with tools and strategies to break the cycle of deceit.

How To Use This Book To Get The Most Out Of These Questions?

"Unraveling Lies: Liberating Yourself From Compulsive Lying By Unmasking The Truth" is more than just a book—it's a therapeutic tool, a companion for your introspective journey.

Here's how to get the most from it:

1. Reserve Quiet Time:

Each question requires introspection and honesty. Dedicate time each day when you can be alone, without distractions. This will allow you to fully engage with each query.

2. Journal Your Responses:

Writing can provide a tangible form to your thoughts and feelings. So record your answers honestly, without judgment or fear. Over time, you'll see patterns and deeper insights.

3. Pace Yourself:

Don't rush through the questions. Each one is a stepping stone towards self-discovery. Some questions might resonate more than others—spend time with them.

4. Embrace the Uncomfortable:

Some questions might trigger discomfort or unease. Remember, these feelings are part of confronting and understanding your lying behavior.

5. Revisit the Questions:

Your perspectives can change over time. So feel free to revisit questions, reflecting on how your answers evolve.

6. Seek Professional Support:

This book can be a catalyst for change but is not a substitute for professional help. If needed, consider seeking a therapist or counselor for further guidance.

This book is your journey toward truth. Remember, it's not about speed, but about transformation. So be patient and kind to yourself as you navigate the maze of introspection.

The path to authenticity begins now.

100 Questions To Liberate Yourself From Compulsive Lying And Get Better

1. Why do I feel the need to lie compulsively?

2. When did I first start lying compulsively?

3. How has compulsive lying affected my relationships?

4. Have I ever experienced negative consequences as a result of my compulsive lying?

5. How do I feel after I lie compulsively?

6. What are the triggers or situations that make me more likely to lie?

7. Have I sought professional help for my compulsive lying?

8. What are the underlying emotions or fears that drive my compulsive lying?

9. How does compulsive lying affect my self-esteem?

10. Have I ever lost friendships or relationships due to my compulsive lying?

11. Do I feel guilty or remorseful after lying compulsively?

12. How does compulsive lying impact my ability to trust others?

13. Do I believe my own lies after a while?

14. Have I noticed any patterns or themes in my lies?

15. What are the potential reasons behind my need for external validation through lies?

16. How does my compulsive lying impact my overall well-being?

17. Have I ever considered the potential long-term consequences of my compulsive lying?

18. Have I lied about significant aspects of my life, such as education, achievements, or experiences?

19. How do I think my compulsive lying affects others?

20. Have I ever tried to stop lying compulsively? If so, what strategies did I use?

21. How do I think my compulsive lying started in the first place?

22. What are the potential triggers for my lying behavior?

23. Have I ever lied about something important that could have legal or ethical consequences?

24. How do I feel when someone catches me in a lie?

25. Have I ever experienced a loss of credibility or reputation due to my compulsive lying?

26. Do I feel like I have control over my lying behavior?

27. Have I ever sought forgiveness from someone I've lied to? How did it go?

28. Do I believe that I can change and overcome my compulsive lying addiction?

29. Have I ever been caught in a web of lies that I couldn't keep up with?

30. How does my compulsive lying affect my ability to build genuine connections with others?

31. Have I lied about my achievements or qualifications to gain advantages in work or education?

32. Do I find it difficult to differentiate between truth and lies at times?

33. Have I ever lied to cover up other addictive behaviors or habits?

34. How has my compulsive lying affected my own sense of identity?

35. Do I feel in control of my lying behavior, or is it compulsive and automatic?

36. How has my lying impacted my personal and professional reputation?

37. Have I ever considered the potential harm I may be causing others through my lies?

38. How do I feel when someone confronts me about my lying behavior?

39. Do I have any regrets about specific lies I have told?

40. Have I ever sought therapy or counseling to address my compulsive lying?

41. How does my lying behavior align with my personal values?

42. Have I lost friendships or opportunities due to my lying behavior?

43. Do I have a support system that understands and helps me through my lying addiction?

44. How do I feel when someone trusts me, knowing I have a history of lying?

45. What are the potential underlying issues or traumas that may contribute to my lying addiction?

46. Do I believe that my lying behavior is a coping mechanism for something deeper?

47. How would my life be different if I could overcome my compulsive lying addiction?

48. Have I ever tried to rationalize or justify my lying behavior?

49. How does my compulsive lying affect my mental and emotional well-being?

50. Have I ever sought accountability for my lying behavior from someone I trust?

51. How do I feel when I see the impact of my lies on others?

52. Have I ever felt powerless or out of control regarding my lying behavior?

53. How has my compulsive lying affected my ability to maintain long-term relationships?

54. Do I find it difficult to be vulnerable and authentic with others due to my lying addiction?

55. Have I ever faced legal consequences as a result of my lying behavior?

56. How do I think my compulsive lying addiction affects my credibility at work or in professional settings?

57. Have I ever experienced a loss of self-respect due to my lying behavior?

58. Do I feel a sense of relief when I lie, or is it followed by anxiety and guilt?

59. How do I think my compulsive lying addiction has impacted my family relationships?

60. Have I ever lied to myself about the extent of my lying addiction?

61. Do I feel a sense of shame or embarrassment about my lying behavior?

62. How has my compulsive lying affected my ability to trust others?

63. Have I ever sought forgiveness from myself for the lies I've told?

64. Do I believe that my lying behavior is changeable, or do I feel stuck in this pattern?

65. Have I ever used manipulation tactics alongside my lying to achieve desired outcomes?

66. How has my compulsive lying affected my overall integrity?

67. Do I find it difficult to remember the truth due to the web of lies I've created?

68. Have I ever felt isolated or lonely due to my lying addiction?

69. How does my lying behavior impact my ability to have genuine, meaningful connections?

70. Do I believe that my lying behavior has caused harm to others, even if unintentionally?

71. How has my compulsive lying affected my reputation within my social circles?

72. Have I ever lied about my emotions or feelings to manipulate a situation?

73. Do I feel a sense of control or power when I lie?

74. How has my lying behavior affected my ability to forgive myself for past mistakes?

75. Have I ever sought validation through my lies, even if temporary?

76. Do I find it challenging to differentiate between lies and reality at times?

77. How does my lying addiction affect my ability to maintain trust with others?

78. Have I ever lied about my past or personal history to create a more desirable narrative?

79. How do I think my compulsive lying addiction affects my self-image?

80. Do I believe I deserve to be honest and authentic with myself and others?

81. How has my lying addiction impacted my ability to set and maintain personal boundaries?

82. Have I ever sought help from a support group or community to address my compulsive lying?

83. How does my lying behavior affect my ability to build a fulfilling and genuine life?

84. Do I feel a sense of satisfaction or accomplishment when I successfully deceive someone?

85. How has my lying addiction affected my mental and emotional well-being over time?

86. Have I ever experienced a loss of personal identity due to the web of lies I've created?

87. Do I believe that my lying behavior is a symptom of deeper emotional wounds?

88. How does my lying addiction affect my ability to make sound decisions?

89. Have I ever lied about my financial situation or resources to gain advantages?

90. How does my lying behavior affect my ability to maintain personal integrity?

91. Do I believe that my lying addiction can be overcome with the right support and effort?

92. Have I ever used lies to manipulate the perceptions others have of me?

93. How has my compulsive lying affected my ability to build trust within myself?

94. Do I feel a sense of relief or liberation when I consider being honest and authentic?

95. How has my lying addiction affected my mental and emotional stability?

96. Have I ever sought guidance from a therapist or counselor to address my lying behavior?

97. How does my lying addiction impact my ability to form healthy and meaningful connections?

98. Do I believe that I can change and grow beyond my compulsive lying addiction?

99. How has my lying behavior affected my ability to forgive myself for past mistakes?

100. Am I ready and willing to take the necessary steps to overcome my compulsive lying addiction?

Conclusion

You've now come to the end of "Unraveling Lies: Liberating Yourself From Compulsive Lying By Unmasking The Truth." Thank you for embarking on this profoundly personal journey.

The strength it took to confront each question with honesty and openness is commendable. I hope this book has been a catalyst for change and self-understanding.

Your journey can now become a beacon of hope for others. Sharing your experiences can shine a light for those navigating similar paths. An Amazon review is an impactful way to share your thoughts and reflections on the book.

Not only does your feedback greatly help me as the author, it can also provide invaluable guidance to potential readers seeking solutions in their lives.

Your words might be the nudge someone needs to begin their journey toward authenticity. So, please take a moment to leave a review on Amazon and share how this book has resonated with you.

Every story matters. Your story matters. And your journey, marked by courage, self-reflection, and transformation, can serve as a beacon for others in their quest for change.

Once again, thank you for trusting this book as your guide, and for stepping into the power of your truth. Here's to your journey and the incredible impact your shared experiences can make in the lives of others.

Wish you the best!

Yakalou

Books By YAKALOU MEDIA

- Questions to Gain Clarity About Your Life
- Questions to Gain Clarity About Your Purpose
- Questions to Gain Clarity About Your Career
- Questions to Ask Yourself to Get Clarity About Your Passions
- Questions to Have Clarity About Your Personal Finance
- Questions to Clarity About Your Relationships with Your Parents
- Questions You Must Ask Yourself When Dating in Your 30s
- 70+ Ways to Ask a Guy or Girl to Be Friends with Benefits (FWB)
- 30 Reasons Why Happily Married Men Cheat
- Questions to Gain Clarity About your Spiritual Beliefs
- Questions to Gain Clarity About Choosing Your Life Partner.
- 100 Questions I Should Ask Myself Before Coming Out
- Questions to Ask Yourself to Get Clarity About Your Mental Health
- Questions To Ask Yourself To Have Clarity About Your Decision-making Process
- Questions To Ask Yourself To Have Clarity About Your Work-life Balance

- 100 Essential Questions to Ask Yourself When Dating in Your Late 20s
- Back to the Dating World: 100 Questions a Single Mom Must Ask Herself
- Questions to Ask Yourself About Sex Addiction When Approaching Your 30s
- 100 Questions to Ask Yourself About Compulsive lying addiction

—Please leave a review!

As always, we value your feedback and would love to read your review of this book!